FAR EAST

589 Wen Ti reunites China

618–907 T'ang Dynasty in China

624 Japan adopts Buddhism

663 Japanese withdraw from Korea

907 Civil war in China

939 Civil wars break out in Japan
960 Sung Dynasty in China

995–1028 Golden age of the arts in Japan

1156 Civil wars ravage Japan
1161 Explosives used in battle in China

1206 Temujin proclaimed Genghis Khan
1210 Mongols begin invasion of China

1271 Marco Polo, the Venetian explorer, travels to Cathay (China)

1368–1644 Ming Dynasty in China

ELSEWHERE

500 Maya and Mochica cultures flourish in Central and South America

750 Toltecs create an empire in the Valley of Mexico

850 Acropolis of Zimbabwe built in eastern Africa

900 Mayas emigrate to Yucatán Peninsula
920–1050 Golden Age of Ghana empire

999 Bagauda, first King of Kano (in Africa)

1077–1087 Almoravid dynasty in Ghana, Africa

1151 End of Toltec empire in Mexico

1189 Last known Norse visit to North America

1240 End of empire of Ghana

1300 Ife kingdom in Nigeria
1325 Aztecs found Tenochtitlán

1438 Inca empire established in Peru

1492 Christopher Columbus discovers the New World

AD 550

700

1000

1490

Don

GREAT CIVILIZATIONS

The Rise of Islam

Contents

Top: A tile showing the Ka'ba, the most holy Muslim building at Mecca. Muslims turn in its direction when they pray. Centre: The Mughal emperor Babur instructs his gardeners. Below: The Court of the Lions in the Alhambra, the great Muslim palace at Granada in Spain. Previous page: A 13th-century Persian tile. Round the edge is a verse from the Koran.

Editorial

Author
Anton Powell

Editor
Frances M. Clapham

Assistant Editor
Elizabeth Wiltshire

Illustrators
Nigel Chamberlain
Richard Hook

LONGMAN GROUP LIMITED
London
Associated companies, branches and representatives throughout the world

First published 1979

Designed and produced by Grisewood & Dempsey Ltd, Grosvenor House, 141–143 Drury Lane, London WC2
© Grisewood & Dempsey Ltd, 1979

Printed and bound by New Interlitho, Milan, Italy

BRITISH LIBRARY CATALOGUING IN PUBLICATION DATA

Powell, Anton
  The rise of Islam. – (Great civilizations; 5).
1. Islamic Empire – History – Juvenile literature.
I. Title   II. Series
909'.09'7671   DS38.3
ISBN 0-582-39051-6

The Rise of Islam

In the 7th century AD a new religion was founded in the desert country of Arabia. It was known as *Islam*, which means 'submission to the Will of Allah (God)'. The followers of this new religion were called Muslims. They believed that it was their duty to spread their new religion as widely as possible. Within less than a hundred years the Arab Muslims ruled an empire which reached from Spain in the west to the borders of India in the east. Later Islam spread to India itself, and still farther east. Today Islam is one of the most important religions in the world.

The Muslims did not only spread their religion. They also spread their ways of life. Their rule led to a vast 'common market' where goods and ideas could be freely exchanged. All over the Muslim empire people lived and worked in much the same way. And they went on doing so after the Muslim Empire had broken up into separate states. Islam lays down many laws concerning everyday things, and in some places these are still followed today.

This book is just a brief introduction to the world of Islam – its religion, its history, and its way of life.

Above: This drug jar was made in Spain in the 15th century. It is decorated with Arabic writing. The Muslims ruled much of Spain from the 8th to the 15th centuries. Below: All over the Islamic world the domes of mosques and slender minarets dominate the skyline. These are in Mashad, in Iran.

وَمِنْهُمْ جَبْرَئِيلُ

world. From their bases on the Mediterranean Sea and the Arabian Gulf, Islamic traders reached northern Europe and China, bringing the attractive goods of their own lands.

'Islam' is the name given to the religion and civilization of Muslims. The word means submission and peace. Muslims believe that there is only one God, Allah, and that the last and greatest of his prophets was Muhammad. The words of Allah, revealed to Muhammad through the archangel Gabriel, are arranged in a holy book called the 'Koran'.

The Prophet and the message
Muhammad himself was an Arab and so were his first followers. He was born in about AD 571 in Mecca, a town in western Arabia. When he was about 25 he married a woman called Khadija, who was about 15 years older than himself. They had several children. Muhammad sometimes went to stay in the lonely mountains around Mecca to think deeply about religion. Muslims believe that during Muhammad's visits to the

The Prophet and Paradise

In the 7th century AD a new religion grew up in Arabia. Its founder was the Prophet Muhammad.

During the early Middle Ages, the civilization of Islam became the most impressive in the world. Lands from Spain to the borders of India were governed by Islamic rulers. The Islamic city of Baghdad was the largest city in the world, and the largest city in western Europe was Cordoba, the capital of Islamic Spain. The luxury in which Islam's rulers lived was famous even in distant Christian lands. The scientists and doctors of Islam were the best in the

Muslims believe that Allah's messenger was the angel Gabriel. He is shown here blowing a trumpet; his wings end in a dragon's head. On his head he wears a turban, like Muslim men on Earth. This painting, which was made in the late 14th century, comes from Baghdad in Iraq.

CHRONOLOGY
571 Muhammad is born in Mecca
610 Muhammad has his first revelation through the angel Gabriel
622 Muhammad and his followers move to Medina (the *Hijra*)
630 The Muslims return to Mecca which becomes the centre of Islam
632 Death of Muhammad
633 The Muslims conquer Syria and Iraq
639 The Muslims begin the conquest of Egypt
640 Persia (Iran) comes under Muslim rule
711 Spain and the Indus Valley are invaded by the Muslims
732 The Muslims are defeated at the battle of Poitiers by Charles Martel, leader of the Franks
750 The Umayyads are overthrown by the 'Abbasids
762 Baghdad becomes the 'Abbasid capital
786 Harun ar-Raschid becomes caliph
970 The Seljuk Turks become Muslims and occupy most of Persia
1055 The Seljuks seize Baghdad
1085 The Christians begin conquest of Spain
1099 Crusaders take Jerusalem
1187 Saladin retakes Jerusalem for the Muslims
1260 Mamluk sultans control Egypt and Syria
1379 Timur the Lame invades Persia
1453 Ottoman Turks capture Constantinople (Byzantium) which becomes their capital
1492 Granada falls to Christians who burn Muslim books and expel Muslims

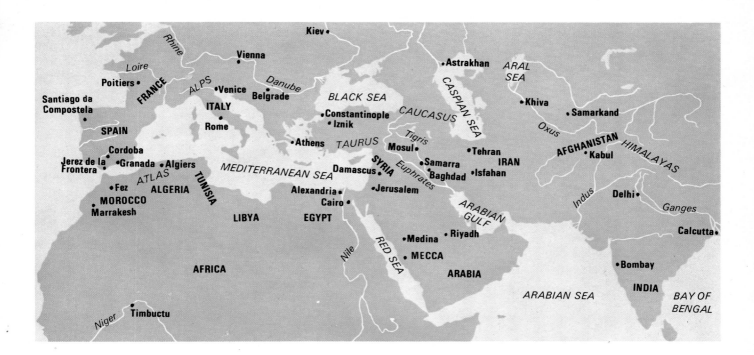

mountains, the angel Gabriel appeared to him and revealed Allah's great message to mankind. This message included commands, warnings about Hell, promises about Paradise, and guidance for everyday life.

The message of Allah, which Muhammad reported, was similar in some ways to Jewish and Christian thought. For instance prophets such as Abraham and Noah, honoured by Jews and Christians, were also respected by the Muslims. But there were many important differences between Muslim belief and the beliefs of Jews and Christians. Jews and Christians did not share the Muslim belief that Muhammad was a great prophet, and Muslims did not accept the Christian belief that Christ was the son of God. Muslims respected Christ as a prophet, but they believed that the teachings of Muhammad were far more important.

From Mecca to Medina

When Muhammad first preached his message in Mecca, many of the townspeople did not believe it. So in AD 622 Muhammad left Mecca, although he took with him some followers who did accept his message. He went to another Arabian town which was soon renamed Medina an-nabi, 'the City of the Prophet'. It was in Medina that Muhammad first attracted a large number of followers and became very powerful. He set up the first Islamic government there, and guided his followers. Muhammad's move from Mecca to Medina is known as the *hijra*. Muslims saw the hijra as the start of a

Mecca is shown in many Muslim pictures, rugs, and tiles. In the centre of this tile, which was made in 1666, is the Ka'ba. It is a cube-shaped building, draped in a black cloth. Inside is the Black Stone which is said to have been given to Abraham by Gabriel. It became the most holy building of Islam.

9

MOSQUES

A building in which Muslims worship is known in Arabic as a *masjid*. This means 'a place for bowing to the ground in worship of Allah'. From masjid comes our word 'mosque'. When praying, men and women have to face in the direction of Mecca, where the sacred Ka'ba is kept (see page 9). Part of the wall of a mosque is specially marked to show this direction. This part is called the *mihrab*, and is often beautifully decorated. Mosques that are used on Fridays, the Muslim holy day, have a stand called a *minbar* for the preacher.

The earliest mosques in Arabia were oblong, in imitation of the house of Muhammad. Later mosques, as in Iran, were much more elaborate, with huge domes and large courtyards. Large mosques have several towers called minarets. From the top of the minaret a man known as a *muezzin* calls worshippers to prayer, his voice carrying over a large area.

new age in history and counted their years from this time. In this book we shall use Christian dates for the sake of simplicity. But we should remember that for Muslims, now and in the past, the hijra is not thought of as happening in the Christian year AD 622. It happened in the Muslim year 1.

Muhammad and his followers were anxious to tell people about the coming of Hell and Paradise, so that they could change their behaviour before it was too late. Muhammad's power grew and much of Arabia came under his control. In 630 he re-entered Mecca. This time he was its ruler.

The Koran

Muslims believe that the words of Allah were dictated to Muhammad by the angel Gabriel a little at a time. He learned them by heart, and repeated them to his followers. Some of them, who could write, took the words down 'on date leaves and pieces of white stone'. Others learned them by heart. They were

Inside the Great Mosque at Damascus in Syria. Mosques, unlike churches, are not decorated with pictures and statues. Instead abstract patterns decorate the walls, while colourful carpets cover the floor on which people pray.

Left: Pilgrimage to Mecca is one of the duties of a good Muslim. The drawings round this doorway include the Ka'ba and other buildings in Mecca; drawings like this often show that the man who lives there has made his pilgrimage.

Below: Pilgrims on the road to Mecca. They make their journey more lively by playing trumpets and drums. The pilgrimage was also a time for trading, and for learning from educated men in the towns along the route. This picture was painted in Baghdad in 1237. It comes from a collection of Arab stories called the 'Maqamat' of al-Hariri.

THE KORAN

The Koran is about the same length as the New Testament of the Christian Bible, roughly 78 thousand words. It is divided into chapters called *suras*. The longest suras come first. These are mostly instructions about daily life. The shortest suras, which come at the end, give warnings about the Day of Judgement, and the terrible fate of people who believe in more than one god. Muslim teaching is based on the Koran, and even today many devout Muslims still learn the whole book by heart.

---

collected into a single book, the Koran. The language of the Koran is Arabic.

Muhammad forbade his followers to write down his own sayings and actions. He did not want them to get muddled up with the message of Allah. After his death, his followers wrote them down. They are called *hadith*, the Traditions. They are used by Muslims as a second source of sacred rules and advice.

Paradise

In AD 632 (the Muslim year 11) Muhammad died, but the power of his message lived on. His followers went on spreading it (see page 12). They were greatly encouraged in this by the promises which Allah had made about Paradise, where good Muslims hoped to go when they died. Paradise is described in the Koran. It is said to contain many things which men must have longed for in the hot, dry, and often lonely lands of Arabia. In Paradise there are 'gardens of dark green' with 'gushing fountains' and plentiful meat. People in Paradise will lie on couches with cushions, on rich carpets, where 'the fruit of the gardens will be close at hand'. As companions in Paradise, good Muslim men will have beautiful women, called *houris*, with 'large, dark eyes' and 'shy glances'.

The rewards of being a faithful Muslim were very attractive. If they were going to earn these rewards, Muhammad's followers believed that they needed to spread his message outside Arabia. This work would be tiring and dangerous. But Islam had to conquer the world.

Conquest and the Caliphate

In less than a hundred years Islam spread to Spain in the west, and to the borders of India in the east, building a vast empire.

The power of Muhammad and his followers meant that Arabia had become the first Islamic country. To the north of Arabia stretched the rich and powerful lands of the Byzantine empire, from North Africa, through Egypt and Syria, to Asia Minor. The Byzantine empire had developed from the Ancient Roman empire. It was ruled from Constantinople (once called Byzantium and now called Istanbul). Its chief religion was Christianity, and its main language was Greek. Shortly after Muhammad's death, his Arabian followers invaded this great foreign territory. What gave them the courage to do so?

The message of Muhammad had given the Arabs a new confidence. Allah had chosen one of their own people, an Arab, to be his great Prophet. Arabs now believed that theirs was the true religion. As Muslims, they felt that they had a right to spread their faith, and that Allah would support them. And if they were killed while fighting for Islam, they might go to Paradise.

A tribal battle between Arabs mounted on camels. The Arabs were very skilled fighters, who would make surprise attacks from the desert and then retreat to it, few enemies daring to follow them there.

Conquering an empire

The Muslim warriors, riding camels and horses, advanced from the deserts of Arabia and began their attack. Great areas of the Byzantine empire surrendered to them amazingly quickly. By 642, only 10 years after the Prophet's death, Syria, Palestine, and Egypt had been conquered. By 661 most of the Byzantine territory in North Africa was under Arab control. In these areas the local people, although Christians, often welcomed the Muslims. Byzantine rule, with its heavy taxes, had been unpopular. One Christian wrote that the Syrians were happy to be rid of 'the wickedness, anger, and cruelty' of the Byzantines.

Eastwards from Syria and Palestine, the Muslim armies moved through lands which had belonged to the Sassanid rulers, enemies of the Byzantines. Iraq, Persia, and Afghanistan were conquered. Far away in the west, Muslim forces from North Africa crossed the Mediterranean in 710, and quickly conquered

---

PERSIA

Persia, or Iran, was a powerful and independent state before the Arabs conquered it. It was ruled by men known as Sassanids. After the conquest the Persians were converted to Islam and later helped to spread it eastwards. They came to use the Arabic script. They kept their own language. In art they continued to paint people and animals, although most Muslims disapproved of this (see page 28). The Mongols invaded Persia in the 13th century and did much damage. Very few paintings have survived from before that time. But paintings from the late 13th century onwards help to give us an idea of Muslim life. Many of the paintings were illustrations to books; they used brilliant colours and were crowded with details. There are several in this book.

WARFARE

Many of the first Muslim soldiers rode camels or horses. Lances, swords and bows and arrows were their favourite weapons. The Bedouin (the Arabs of the desert) took their bows and arrows with them almost everywhere. Shirts made of mail (metal links) or of leather gave protection against enemy weapons. Arabs often defeated their enemies in battle by pretending to be beaten, and riding away. When the enemy chased after them in careless excitement, the Arabs turned, and made an unexpected, deadly attack.

The Arabs quickly learned how to capture enemy towns by watching how their Byzantine and Persian opponents fought. They learned how to knock down walls with battering rams and with stones hurled from great catapults. Sometimes miners dug tunnels under enemy walls to make them collapse. Enemy prisoners were probably ordered to build for the Arabs the sort of machines that the enemy used against towns. Movable wooden towers were made for the Arabs. With soldiers inside, they were pushed up to the enemy walls. The Muslim soldiers could jump across.

At sea, too, the Muslims copied the Byzantines. They built large wooden warships, which were driven by a hundred or more armed rowers. They learned from the Byzantines how to make and use 'Greek fire' or naphtha. Naphtha was a substance thrown at enemy ships and buildings to set them on fire. Burning naphtha was very difficult to put out. When it landed on human flesh, the effect was terrible.

much of Spain. France was their next target, but here at last the Muslim advance stopped at Poitiers when their armies were defeated by the Franks in 732. Forces led by the Arabs were also beaten off in the east, near Constantinople, in 747. Much later (between 1014 and 1025) Islam spread to northern India. By the early 8th century a massive area of Islamic rule had already been formed, stretching from Spain in the west to the borders of India in the east.

Umayyads and 'Abbasids

Muhammad ruled the first Muslims in Arabia as both military and religious leader. The great Islamic empire, in its early years, was ruled by a succession of *caliphs*, men who were seen as inheriting Muhammad's power of command, though not his power of prophecy. The first caliphs were related to Muhammad, or had been his companions. Between 660 and 750 the caliph was always a member of the clan called the Umayyads. But many Muslims came to feel that the Umayyads were unsuitable successors to Muhammad. After a bloody revolt in 750 they lost their power.

The new ruling clan was called the 'Abbasids. Their general, 'Abdullah,

feared that the Umayyads might somehow regain power. So he invited all the surviving Umayyads to a feast, and when nearly all of them had arrived, he had them executed. Then, the story goes, he spread leather covers over the bodies, and went on with the feast, although the groans of the dying Umayyads could still be heard. Later 'Abdullah himself came to a bad end. He rebelled against his 'Abbasid caliph, but was captured. The

The citadel at Aleppo in Syria was one of the strongest fortresses in the Arab world. Even so it was destroyed and rebuilt several times. This part was built by Ghazi, son of the 12th-century ruler Saladin who was one of the greatest Muslim battle leaders.

13

'Abbasids enclosed him in a house specially built of salt, with its foundations near water. When the water had eaten away the salt foundations, the house collapsed and 'Abdullah was buried alive, as the 'Abbasids planned.

The first 'Abbasid caliphs tried to show that they were not like the Umayyads. In the 750s they moved the capital of Islam from Damascus in Syria, where the Umayyads had reigned, eastwards to Iraq. Here at Baghdad a vast new city was built, where the 'Abbasid caliphs reigned in splendour until 1258. In that year the last caliph of Baghdad was killed by Mongol invaders from the east who destroyed the city.

The 'Abbasids tried to make their subjects obedient by claiming that the caliph was specially favoured by Allah. One caliph said, 'Anyone who disobeys us is disobeying Allah, and Allah will send him to Hell'. But several of the caliphs' territories, such as Spain, North Africa, and Egypt, broke away from 'Abbasid control, and set up Muslim governments of their own. Even in Baghdad, the caliphs had lost much of their power by AD 900.

Non-Arab Muslims

In the first centuries of Islam, many millions of people outside Arabia were converted to the Muslim religion. Eventually these non-Arab Muslims far outnumbered the Arabs. The Koran stated that all good Muslims were equal in the sight of Allah. But the Umayyad caliphs had discriminated against the new Muslims who were not Arabs, by refusing to appoint them to positions of honour.

This discrimination was resented by the non-Arabs. Many of them were just as proud of their ancestors as the Arabs were of theirs. One non-Arab Muslim from Persia is said to have boasted to an Umayyad caliph in these words: 'My ancestors were princes. They defeated the rulers of the Turks and the Greeks. They stalked in heavy coats of mail, like ravenous lions. We Persians are descended from a race which is better than all others.' But the Umayyad caliph himself was of Arab, and not Persian, descent. He was so angry at this boast that he threw the man into a pond where he nearly drowned. The non-Arab Muslims helped to overthrow the Umayyads. Under the 'Abbasid caliphs they were allowed much more power.

At the start of the Islamic empire, the Arab rulers usually treated their new subjects in a gentle and tolerant way. Few were forced to become Muslims. But people who were not Muslims did have to pay a special tax. At one time, so many people were becoming Muslims, in order to avoid paying this tax, that the caliph became anxious to stop some of them. He was losing too much money.

Christians and Jews

Many of the Christians and Jews who lived in the Islamic world were not willing to become Muslims. As a result

Among the regions soon conquered by the Muslims was the Holy Land around Jerusalem. Many Christian pilgrims flocked there, and sometimes came into conflict with the Muslims, or Saracens as they called them. The Christians launched great campaigns called Crusades against the Muslims. They wanted to take control of the Bible Lands themselves, but were only successful for brief periods. The Crusades were very important to Europeans but to the Muslims they were just border wars. Just before 1300 the Christians were driven out of the Holy Land. In this picture of a battle between Muslims and Crusaders, the Crusaders are wearing the sign of the Cross.

they were usually treated by Muslim rulers as inferior people. Sometimes they were insulted. One caliph ordered Christians and Jews to fix little models of the devil to their houses, so that good Muslims would not go near them. But usually Christians and Jews were left in peace. Muslim rulers were far more tolerant than the Christian rulers of Europe in their treatment of other religions. In Christian lands in the Middle Ages Jews and Christians with unusual beliefs were often simply murdered. At the end of the Middle Ages, when Christians conquered the Muslims of Spain, they treated them very badly indeed (see page 41).

As a result of Muslim tolerance, Jews and Christians were able to add to the achievements of Islam. Many of the great thinkers, scientists, and doctors of Islamic lands were of course Muslims, but many others were Christians or Jews. Muslims borrowed and improved on several of the best ideas of non-Muslim societies: ideas for science, medicine, and even for religious building. The civilization of Islam was a blend of ideas from many lands. But the main language of this civilization was Arabic, the language which the companions of Muhammad had brought with them from the desert.

THE TURKS

In the early days of Islam the Muslim lands were ruled by a caliph of Arab descent. But many provinces came to be governed by their own rulers, or sultans. Some of them came from Persian families, and some – who came to dominate the Islamic world – were Turks.

The Turks were originally nomads from the steppes of central Asia. At first they came into the Islamic world as slaves, who were converted to Islam and formed its most important soldiers. The Mamluks who ruled Egypt from the 13th century were descended from Turkish slaves. Later free Turkish tribes migrated into Muslim areas and were converted.

In the 11th century the Seljuk Turks won lands from the Byzantines in Asia Minor – the area which is now called Turkey after them and their successors, the Ottoman Turks. In 1453 the Ottomans captured Constantinople, the last tiny remnant of the once great Byzantine empire. From then on they ruled a vast empire which reached into Europe, along the coast of North Africa, and included Egypt and much of the Near East. It fell only in the 20th century.

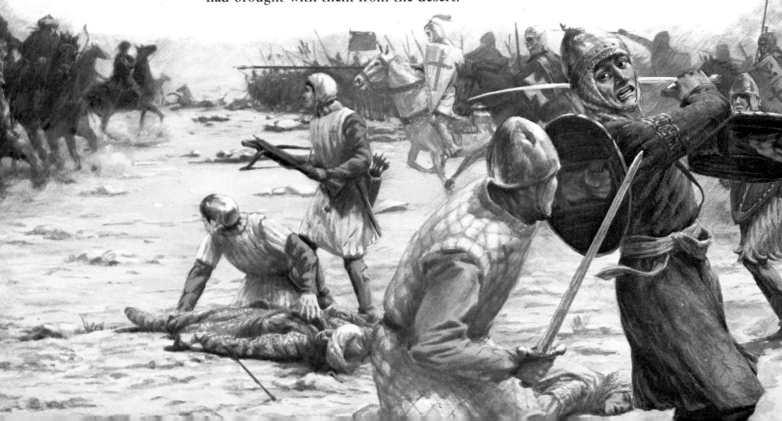

Life at Court

The courts of Islamic rulers were places of fantastic luxury and extravagant entertainment.

Rulers gained huge sums of money from the taxes of Muslim lands. Part of this money was used for the needs of the ruler's subjects, but much of it was used to provide luxuries for the ruler himself, and to look after his servants. In AD 918–919 the caliph at Baghdad had an income from his territories of about $14\frac{1}{2}$ million gold dinars. Of this, 14 million dinars were spent on the caliph's court and on government employees in Baghdad. Very little was spent on the rest of the caliph's empire.

The palace of an Islamic ruler was often a large community, with thousands of slaves and servants living nearby. In Egypt and Spain palaces were built away from the main city, so that the ruler would not be troubled by the riots of poor and discontented citizens. Another advantage of living near the countryside was that the ruler could easily enjoy outdoor sports, such as polo, horse-racing, and hunting. Carefully trained and highly valued animals were used for hunting. A favourite breed of royal hunting dog was the saluki, which came originally from Saluq in southern Arabia. One Umayyad caliph, Yazid I, decorated his hunting dogs with gold ornaments around their ankles. Cheetahs, the fastest animals in the world over short distances, were also used for hunting. Yazid's cheetah was trained to ride to the hunt perched on horseback.

Musicians and dancers at the wedding of a powerful Muslim in India, in the 15th century. The Prophet Muhammad was believed to have disapproved of musical instruments, saying that they were 'the devil's muezzin'. But many people became skilled in their use and music was a part of festivals and gatherings in villages and in courts. The dancers have castanets, which Muslims introduced to Spain where they are now part of the musical tradition.

Left: The invention of backgammon. Men at court entertained themselves by playing games. The story goes that the King of India sent a chess set to the Persian ruler, who ordered his vizier to invent an equally complicated game in reply. His answer was backgammon, a game that is still played in the Near East today.

The Indian ruler Babur gives instructions to his gardeners. High walls of mudbrick shut out strangers, and kept out sand from the desert. Rich men made beautiful gardens that were like works of art. Flowers glowed with colour and filled the air with their scent, and pools and fountains gave a feeling of coolness. They spent a great deal of time in their gardens, sitting on carpets (which were often designed to look like gardens themselves) and eating and playing games with their friends. Muslims thought that Paradise would be a beautiful garden.

The Court of the Lions in the palace of the Alhambra at Granada in Spain was built in the late 14th century. The central fountain is carried by 12 bronze lions. It comes from an 11th-century palace on the same site. Around the courtyard delicate columns hold up arches in the Moorish (North African) style.

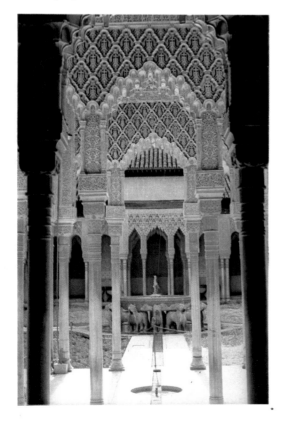

Entertaining at court

Inside the palace, the ruler and his courtiers were entertained by singers, dancers, and musicians. An especially impressive display was put on when the ambassador of a foreign state arrived, to show the ambassador how rich and powerful the ruler was. The furnishings of an Islamic palace were often superb. Around three sides of the palace rooms was a low couch, called a diwan. Food was served on tables by the diwan, or on cushions on the floor. These cushions were placed on carpets woven in complicated and colourful patterns. More carpets were hung on the walls.

Food at court could be extremely expensive. Chickens were fed on milk and almonds to make their flesh delicate. Watermelons for the caliph at Baghdad were brought hundreds of miles across the desert, preserved in lead cases which were packed with ice from lands far to the north-east. A favourite drink, especially with court

17

An outdoor reception in a Mughal palace in India. This picture was painted in the 18th century, and shows how little ways of life had changed. The Mughal empire of India was founded by Babur, a descendant of Timur, in the 16th century. Many Indians became Muslims and took up the Islamic way of life. Mughal rulers were great builders, and the Taj Mahal, one of the most famous buildings in the world, was built by one of them as a tomb for his much-loved wife.

This Persian painting shows the great Mongol leader Timur the Lame being entertained near Samarkand. His camp was famous for its splendour. The Mongols, who came from the steppes of Asia, swept down through the Islamic world in the 13th century. They captured Baghdad and its lands and set up new states. But in turn many of them were converted to Islam. Timur, who is also known as Tamerlane, ruled a vast empire from Samarkand from 1370 to 1405.

ladies, was sherbet, made by mixing water sweetened with sugar with the juices of fruit and flowers.

Power and luxury made several of the caliphs intensely proud. Some thought themselves too grand even to obey important Islamic rules, just as some popes and churchmen disobeyed many important Christian rules. The Koran forbids alcoholic drink. But some early caliphs and their courtiers drank heavily. The caliph al-Walid II in the 8th century is reported to have swum in an artificial pond filled with wine. He drank so much, it is said, that the level of the pond went down sharply. (Alcoholic drink was often sold to Muslims by Christians and Jews, people whose religions did not forbid alcohol.)

Pleasures of the rich

Al-Mustansir, an 11th-century ruler of Egypt, owned many beautiful things including chess sets made with gold and silver, and ink stands of precious ebony and ivory. At the court of al-Mu'tamid in Spain, money was spent in a similarly extravagant way. The story is told that one day al-Mu'tamid's wife, I'timad, was delighted by the unusual sight of snow falling at Cordoba. So, to please her, al-Mu'tamid had the surrounding mountains planted with almond trees, which blossom in winter and look like snow. On another occasion I'timad saw some dairy women lifting their skirts to walk through a muddy street. She decided that she would like to copy them, only more elegantly. She would not walk in a muddy street. Instead, large quantities of perfume, rose water, and spices were poured into the courtyard of the palace for her to paddle in.

Stories of expensive living at Islamic courts were no doubt exaggerated by enemies of the rulers. They probably wanted to persuade people that the rulers were behaving wastefully and were not good Muslims. But it is certain that some Muslim rulers enjoyed wild activities, in courts equipped with extremely beautiful and costly furnishings.

Literature

Poems and stories were an important part of entertainment both in courts and in villages.

One of the greatest pleasures at an Islamic court was listening to and composing poetry. Great poets were highly respected. Umayyad caliphs loved to hear poems about the deserts of Arabia, where their ancestors had lived.

Desert poetry was often sad. Sometimes a poem told of an abandoned camp, where a happy group of the poet's friends had once been, but which was now just a lonely ruin. Other poems described a poet's longing for a woman far away.

Arabic poetry also told of warfare, and of the tough men who had led desert raids. One poem described a warrior:

His voice echoes, deep and strong,
among his companions on the raid.
With bare legs, and strong sinews on his
arms, he dashes into the darkest nights
under sheets of rain.

The poor people of the desert were sometimes mentioned: servants, dirtied by work and with rough hands, who looked after the camels, and thin men of the mountains, who climbed in search of wild honey.

One of the greatest Persian poems tells of the exploits of the hero Rustam. Here he is lassooing the emperor of China, and dragging him off his elephant. Rustam is shown wearing a helmet, covered by the face of a snow leopard, and a tiger-skin coat.

This Persian painting is dated 1307. It comes from a book of fables. Here the hare outwits the lion by persuading it to lean over a well to look at its reflection. Encouraged by the hare, the lion leans so far that it falls in.

The collection of stories called the *Arabian Nights* became famous as far as Christian Europe. It included the colourful and exaggerated tales of Sindbad the Sailor. One story told of sailors who landed on a sandy island with trees, and lit a fire. Too late the sailors found that the 'island' was gliding down into the depths of the sea. It was really a great sea-monster, which had floated on the surface so long that trees had grown on it. But it now felt the fire and dived, taking the men with it.

Literature of the Persians

The Persians were very fond of long poems telling of the legendary exploits of heroes, among them Alexander the Great. The deeds of the Mongol leader Timur the Lame were also turned into poems. They also wrote history and geography books. The Persians wrote in their own language, which many Muslims learned so that they could enjoy Persian literature.

Many people in the Islamic world could neither read nor write. But they knew the stories and poems through listening to travelling story-tellers who visited their villages and towns.

Daily Life

As the Arabs conquered, they took with them their language and the Islamic rules for everyday life.

Most Muslims lived very differently from rulers and courtiers. But we know far less about them, since ordinary lives make less exciting reading and few people until today have bothered to record them. Certainly many Muslims were very poor, struggling anxiously to get housing and enough food. Many poor people lived in the countryside, growing crops and raising animals. Some Arab tribes, the Bedouin, lived a wandering life, living in tents and moving with their herds and flocks in search of grazing.

Markets and shopkeepers
Much of the food produced by workers in the country was sold to traders in the towns. These traders then resold it in their shops. Trading was one of the liveliest, and noisiest, activities in a Muslim town. Near the centre of the town was a market made up of covered

The wandering Arabs of the countryside and desert are known as Bedouin. Then, as now, they lived in tents and brought their flocks to market. Here some Bedouin, in their traditional dress, separate their flock for market into sheep and goats.

streets, shops, and stalls. This was called a *suq* in Arabic, and a *bazar* in Persian. Here traders sold their goods, and often had workshops. They would group together, according to their wares; cloth merchants would be in one little street, spice sellers in another, and so on. Traders shouted advertisements for their goods, while men with pack-animals pushed their way through the crowded streets. There were strong smells of cooking, of fish, of vegetables and fruit.

Shopkeepers were forbidden to cheat customers or to sell bad products. Prices were fixed, so that shopkeepers should not make too much profit. An official called a *muhtasib* inspected shops and traders. He made sure that they were trading fairly and not overcharging. One man wrote advice to muhtasibs: he said that they should not allow shopkeepers to put water in milk. He also advised that a special watch should be kept on the men

The 'madrasa' of Ulan Beg at Samarkand. A madrasa was a teaching college, particularly of theology and law. Samarkand was the greatest city of Central Asia, and the Mongol ruler Ulan Beg built his madrasa in the early 15th century. Probably astronomy formed an important part of the studies here; Ulan Beg also built an important observatory, and his star tables were a very important contribution to astronomy.

who sold fried cheese. They should only use fresh oil when cooking it.

In Egypt, a shopkeeper caught charging too high prices was forced to ride through the streets on a camel, carrying a notice which described his crime and ringing a bell to make people look. Probably the crowds had fun shouting and throwing things at him. Traders themselves could protest, if they thought that prices were too low and that they were not making enough profit. Sometimes they arranged a strike, keeping all shops closed for a day or two.

Workers of different kinds organized themselves into associations called *qarmats*. The members of a qarmat were often proud of their work. Christians and Jews were allowed to join, as well as Muslims. Christians and Jews usually lived in separate districts from the Muslims. Muslim rulers did not want

Muslims and non-Muslims to meet very often. They were afraid that the Muslims might copy non-Muslim behaviour, and lose their religious faith. But even in Muslim districts housing for the poor was scarce. In some places people who had no houses turned to squatting, living in empty buildings without permission.

In crowded towns, where there was not enough room to build houses very wide, they were made tall instead. Sometimes they were five or six storeys high. Some of the narrow streets running between these high buildings got very little sunlight, and needed artificial lighting even in the daytime. Wealthy people liked to have town houses built around a courtyard. A door from the street led into the courtyard, where there was often a fountain playing, and a fruit tree. The rooms of the house opened off this courtyard.

In the bazaar, or suq. In booths along the walls tradesmen and their customers talked, and sometimes argued, for a long time before agreeing on a price. Holes in the roof let in shafts of light.

وفي الميادين بالميادين فلا أمين ولا أمين

Left: Another picture from the 1237 'Maqamat'. It shows an imam preaching in a mosque, from the top of a minbar. An old woman, with bent back, walks towards him. Behind her can be seen a decorated mihrab. Below left: An old man prays in the Great Mosque at Damascus.

THE DUTIES OF A MUSLIM

Faithful Muslims still base their lives on a system of beliefs and customs that rest on what are known as the Five Pillars of Islam. These are faith, prayer, almsgiving, fasting, and pilgrimage.

The faith of the Muslims is summed up by the *shahada*. This is the declaration made by people when they join the faith: There is no God but Allah, and Muhammad is His Prophet. Muslims also believe in the Koran as the Word of Allah; in angels as instruments of Allah's will; and in a final Day of Judgement for all people.

Muslims pray at five special times every day. When they pray, they face in the direction of Mecca. The times for prayer are announced by a religious official known as a *muezzin*, who calls from a *minaret*, or tall tower. Close to the minaret is a *mosque*, a building where men and women can pray. The man who leads the prayers at the mosque is called an *imam*. Prayers are commonly said at home, at work, and in the open air.

The sacred day in the Muslim week is Friday (not Sunday, sacred for Christians, or Saturday, sacred for Jews). On Fridays it is especially important for Muslims to gather at the mosque for prayer. Mosques may also be used as courts and schools; justice and education are thought to be part of religion.

The ninth month of the Muslim year is known as Ramadan. It is a time for fasting, when Muslims do not eat or drink anything or smoke between sunrise and sunset.

All Muslims who can should go on a pilgrimage to Mecca and Medina once in their lives. This pilgrimage takes place at a special time of year, and is known as the *hajj*.

Travellers arrive at a village. On the right a woman is drawing out woollen thread with a spindle and in the background are a minaret and the domed top of a mosque. This picture comes from the 'Maqamat' of al-Hariri.

Dress and manners

The *muhtasib* had the job of making sure that people behaved themselves in public. He could punish anyone who did not dress properly. The proper dress for 'Abbasid townsmen included a long, collarless shirt, baggy trousers, and a turban. A loose overgarment covered the whole body. Countrymen often wore long robes, with a shawl covering the head. Townswomen commonly had plain robes with a flowing overgarment. They always covered their heads and in public veiled their faces. Some men tried to look much younger than they really were in the hope of attracting women. This was forbidden, and so a middle-aged man was not allowed to dye his grey beard black. People were sometimes told that it was bad manners to make many jokes and to gossip. They were advised not to eat quickly, lick their fingers, chew garlic or onions (which made their breath smell), use a toothpick in public, or wear clothes that were dirty or patched.

A ploughman with two buffalo. The animals drag the ploughshare which digs up the ground ready for sowing. This picture was painted in Persia in the early 16th century.

FOOD AND DRINK
Muslims' food varies very widely, according to the country they live in. Few things to eat were forbidden by law, but among them were all parts of the pig. Other animals (except flesh-eaters) were allowed, but had to be killed in a special way. All kinds of alcoholic drinks were forbidden.

Muslims flavoured their food with spices and were very fond of sticky sweets, often made with nuts and honey. The custom of following a meat course with something sweet spread from Muslim lands into Europe.

Women

Islamic rules protected women and instructed them to behave modestly.

We know very little about the lives of ordinary women in the early Islamic world. Historians were men, and wrote mostly about rich men and rulers. The women that they did mention were unusual ones, many of them rich and noble.

The Koran gave rules for the behaviour of women, and for the way in which they should be treated. Some of its teachings seem to limit women's freedom very strictly. But we must remember that the Koran dates from the 7th century – more than 1300 years ago. In some ways the Koran's teachings promised women a better position than they had before, or were to have in other societies for centuries to come.

Until the coming of Islam, for example, men in Arabia sometimes had many wives. The Koran allowed a man to have up to four wives, although it was thought better only to have one. A woman could only have one husband. Sometimes a man's wives were jealous of one another, but sometimes they were friends and enjoyed one another's company.

Women at home

A Muslim girl generally married when she was in her early 'teens. Her husband was often chosen by her father. The Koran stated that it was the man's duty to provide for the women in his family, while it was a woman's duty to look after her husband, her children, and their home. A good woman should be obedient to her husband; if not, the Koran said, he could tell her off and even beat her. It was very important that women should behave modestly; grown-up women, both married and unmarried, veiled their faces when they were in public. Country people were less obedient to this law, and went about their work in the fields unveiled, but women who lived in towns wore the veil and tried to appear in public as little as

Two pictures of Persian life in the 16th century. They show a woman churning, and another pounding grain. Women were expected to work hard.

Left: This Persian painting, dated 1529, shows Queen Shirin of Armenia playing polo against Khusraw, King of Persia. The story of Shirin and Khusraw was very popular. This picture is surprising to people who have always thought that all Muslim women led a life shut away in the home.

24

Many Muslim women became very shy. There is a story of a doctor in Baghdad who used shock treatment to cure a young woman suffering from hysterics. He pretended that he was going to have her undressed in front of men. The shock of hearing this was so great that the woman was cured of her illness. To have her body looked at by men was one of the most dreadful things a Muslim woman could imagine.

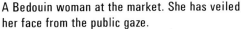
Right: A 'qadi', a judge or magistrate, settles an argument between a father and daughter. The Koran gave women important rights over property.

A Bedouin woman at the market. She has veiled her face from the public gaze.

possible. They were taught to avoid men, except for very close relatives. Spare time should be spent quietly at home.

Women and property
Since it was a man's duty to provide for the women of his family, Muslims were taught to leave twice as much property to their sons (who had women to look after) as to their daughters. On the other hand, a Muslim wife was not obliged to hand over anything she might earn to her husband. When she married, the bridegroom gave her a dowry. This was her own property and it remained hers if her husband divorced her. For centuries the Koran's teachings about women and property meant that they were better looked after than in non-Muslim countries where all a woman's property became her husband's when she got married!

Divorce was possible for Muslims, although it was not encouraged. Muhammad said 'Of all the things Allah has permitted, the one He most dislikes is divorce.'.

Women and learning
In material things men were looked on as more important than women, since they were thought of as the providers. In other respects the Koran teaches that men and women are equal. For instance women, suitably protected, made pilgrimages to Mecca. In early Islam, some women were allowed to study, and some became famous writers and teachers. One even gave talks on literature to large audiences in one of the main Baghdad mosques. Some early Islamic noblewomen are said to have had great power, and even to have led troops into battle.

For most women, life in Islamic countries was probably one of hard work in the house or in the fields. Women's life was also different from one part of the Islamic world to another, for a people's customs would not all be changed when they were converted to Islam.

Slaves

Slavery was discouraged by the Koran, but slaves played an important part in Islamic countries. Some rose to become rulers.

In Muhammad's time slavery was common in the Near East. The Koran, like the Old Testament of the Jews and Christians, allowed slavery but discouraged it. Instead the Koran encouraged Muslims to free their slaves.

Despite this, slaves were used in huge numbers in the Muslim world. Many of them did domestic work or were trained as soldiers. Others, less lucky, were used for digging irrigation trenches, mining for gold and silver, and for working the plantations.

SOURCES OF SLAVES

When the Turkish empire was expanding, battle captives were a good source of slaves. But in later days captives were scarce. Muslims were forbidden to make fellow Muslims slaves, so instead they turned to the sultan's subjects in Albania, Romania, and Greece.

Every now and then, when slaves were running short, a *devshirme* took place. A team headed by a Janissary officer would go around from one village to another. Boys and young men between 10 and 20 were paraded, and the best of them would be taken back to Turkey.

Some of the boys became palace slaves. They were taught the faith of Islam; Turkish; Arabic because it was the language of the Koran; and Persian because the greatest poetry and literature were in that language. They were also taught history and how to fight. The best of them were sent out as provincial governors, and some slaves even rose to be the sultan's vizier, or chief minister. Other slaves joined the Janissaries.

The slave trade

Islam did not allow Muslims, Christians, or Jews to be turned into slaves if they had been born free. So slaves were imported from pagan lands outside the Islamic world. Christians and Jews, as well as Muslims, took part in the slave trade. Black slaves were brought from Africa south of the Sahara. White slaves were often pagan Turks from the lands in the east of the empire, or people from central and northern Europe.

Many of the men were used for heavy labour. Other male slaves were employed as soldiers to guard rulers. Caliphs and others hoped that by using foreign slaves as bodyguards they would be safe against attacks from their own subjects. Many rulers came to regret the use of these bodyguards. The foreign slaves often became too powerful for their masters. At Baghdad, from the 9th century, the 'Abbasid caliphs were controlled by their own Turkish bodyguards, who were fierce soldiers. One of the caliph's subjects wrote a poem to insult them, saying that he could not bear to see these foreign slaves riding proudly round:

The slave market. The Koran allowed slavery, but encouraged slave owners to set their slaves free. It was forbidden to make other Muslims slaves. But slaves did play an important part, as workers and as soldiers. Some of them were prisoners of war, and others came from Africa. This picture of a slavemarket in the Yemen was painted in 1237.

The free men have passed away, they are dead and gone: time has left me among barbarians.

People tell me, 'You are staying at home too much.' But I say it gives me no pleasure to go out.

Whom would I see around me? Only apes riding on horseback.

Soldiers who had been slaves also became rulers in Egypt and Spain.

Some male slaves were forced to be castrated, although this was against the teachings of Islam. 'Eunuchs', as these men were called, were then unable to become the fathers of children. They could safely be used to look after the harems in which Muslim rulers kept their many slave women.

Most of the 'Abbasid caliphs had a slave mother. The nobility of a child was believed to descend from its father. It was not thought to matter if the mother was a foreign slave.

Many attractive female slaves were bought by wealthy citizens. Once a slave woman had borne a child to her master he had a duty to look after her and was not allowed to sell her. When he died she became a free woman.

Slaves with talent

Slave girls who were talented at music, dancing or singing were sometimes specially educated so that they could be sold as entertainers for a ruler's court. Some of these girls became very famous and expensive. It was said that the ideal slave girls were Berbers (from North Africa), who had been taken from their homeland at the age of nine. They needed to go to the slave-school at Medina to learn courtly behaviour, and then to Iraq to learn poetry and music.

One clever slave girl, I'timad, became the wife of the ruler al-Mu'tamid in 11th century Spain. It is said that she first attracted his attention one day when she was washing clothes. Al-Mu'tamid was passing by with a friend making up poetry. The friend reached a difficult point in his poem and could not think how to continue it. Then with amazement the two men heard I'timad

continuing the poem with lines of perfect verse which she had made up on the spot. Al-Mu'tamid took her to his court and later freed her from slavery so that he could marry her. But Al-Mu'tamid lost his position as ruler and was imprisoned in Morocco. I'timad and his daughters stayed with him in his poverty, earning a humble living by spinning.

The treatment of slaves

In some ways slaves were protected. If they committed a crime, they were not supposed to be punished as severely as free people. Very expensive slaves, such as trained singers and dancers, must often have been well looked after. Badly treated slaves might not perform properly, and then their owners would not get good value for the money they had paid for them.

Far less fortunate were the large numbers of slave women bought only for their good looks. As they grew older, many were neglected by their owners. Perhaps unluckier still were the gangs of slave labourers, working in extreme heat or darkness, who were ordered from one harsh job to another on the land and in the mines.

Some slaves became very powerful. This 16th-century painting shows the Turkish Sultan Suleiman on campaign in Hungary. On his right, wearing tall white headdresses and white-skirted uniforms, are some Janissaries. These slaves were excellent soldiers and remained immensely powerful until they were overthrown in the 19th century by the Sultan.

THE JANISSARIES

In the late 14th century the sultan of Turkey needed more troops to control his empire as it grew bigger. He decided to recruit them from his many captives. These new soldiers were called the *Janissaries*, from the Turkish word for 'new forces'. Later, when battle captives became few, the Janissaries were recruited from Christian slaves.

The Janissaries were fierce and brave soldiers. In peacetime they staffed frontier towns and were the police force of the capital Istanbul (formerly Constantinople). They were organized into divisions each with its own symbol – a fish, a key, and so on. Sometimes the men were tattooed with this symbol. Their officers all had titles taken from the kitchen, among them soup-man, water carrier, and black scullion. The great copper cauldrons in which their food was cooked were as precious to the Janissaries as the standard was to ordinary soldiers. When they were unhappy with their conditions they would kick these cauldrons over.

The conditions of the Janissaries were good. They were highly paid, and each time a new sultan came to the throne they demanded a large sum of money for their loyalty. They became so powerful that they helped to overthrow several sultans. At their greatest, in the 15th and 16th centuries, the Janissaries were thought to be unbeatable.

This carpet was made in Cairo in the 16th century. Carpets played many parts in Islamic life. Some, like this, were large and elaborate; the finest were made of silk instead of the coarser wool. This carpet has a central medallion surrounded by other traditional shapes like the eight-pointed star. Some showed gardens of flowers. Fine carpets covered the floors of mosques and palaces. Small rugs were used by people praying. The design in the centre was in the shape of a mihrab, the niche in a mosque wall showing the direction of Mecca. Other rugs were used by nomads as saddle bags, and to decorate the walls of their tents.

Art and Architecture

Mosques and houses in Islamic countries were decorated with beautiful and colourful objects.

The countryside around Muslim towns usually contained few bright colours. To make up for this, people in the towns tried hard to make life very colourful indeed. Shimmering clothes of many different colours were fashionable for men. And the insides of buildings were often decorated and furnished with beautiful designs.

In their designs, the artists and craftsmen of Islam did not often show the figures of human beings or animals. It was thought that only Allah had the right to design such figures, because only he had the power to give them life. A human artist who dared to show these figures would receive a terrible punishment from Allah after his death. Most Islamic art shows patterns which were not meant to look like anything living. Plants and stars were also shown. A few artists, especially in Iran, did dare to show human and animal figures. But several of these appeared as half-hidden by other details of the design. The artists seemed almost ashamed of showing them. Although much of their work was excellent, artists and craftsmen in Islam did not usually sign works.

Brilliant decorations

Islamic countries had very few trees, and so had little wooden furniture. People usually sat and slept on the floor. Fine-looking and comfortable carpets, woven from wool and silk, were therefore in great demand. They were often designed in highly complicated patterns. Many showed elaborate gardens full of flowers.

Other artists decorated walls with glazed (shiny) tiles of many colours and

This mosque lamp comes from Syria, where the first glass was made almost a thousand years before the birth of Christ. The Muslims took up and improved on the skills and art of the regions they conquered, and spread them through the Islamic world.

with mosaics. Mosaics were designs made up of small pieces of differently coloured paste, and of glass with gold around the edges, which were fixed to the wall with plaster. Mosaics had long been made in the Byzantine empire. Craftsmen from there were paid to make them in Islamic countries, and to teach Muslims the art. The use of colour led to brightly painted and glazed pottery, while metal objects were often made using combinations of gold, copper, and silver. Favourite patterns and ways of decorating objects spread all through the Muslim world.

Writing as decoration

Muslims believed that human beings should not be worshipped. Allah, and his words in the Koran, were far more important. This was another reason why Muslim artists did not often show human figures or make statues. Instead, many preferred to beautify the message of

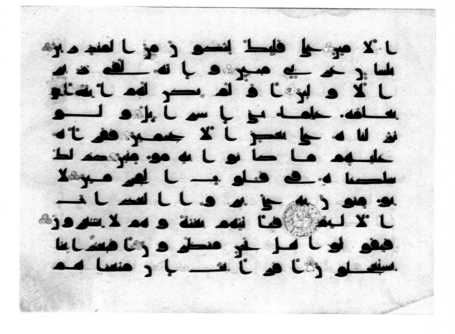

This page from the Koran was probably written in the 9th century. The angular script (style of writing) is called Kufic. It is named after the town of Kufah, near Baghdad, which was an important early Islamic centre of art and learning. Beautiful writing, or calligraphy, was considered a great art; it was used to decorate buildings, glass, and everyday objects as you can see on this page.

The brightly coloured dome of a mosque at Samarra in Iraq. In the distance is a minaret, built around the year 850. Different countries built their minarets in different styles. This minaret, with its spiral ramp, was probably copied from the ancient Mesopotamian buildings called ziggurats. The town of Samarra was built by an 'Abbasid caliph who wanted to escape from mutinous troops in Baghdad.

Allah. Several kinds of *calligraphy* (fine writing) were used to show the words of the Koran in books and also on buildings and pottery. The shapes of the Arabic letters were changed in many ways to make them more beautiful and impressive. As a result of this, the words sometimes became almost impossible to read. But good Muslims would know the words of the Koran by heart, and Allah, who knew everything, would be able to read them.

Domed mosques

Few buildings now survive from early Islamic times. Clay was commonly used for building, and over the years it has crumbled away. The best and longest-lasting building material is stone and it was used mainly for mosques. Christian churches were often taken down, and their stones reused to build mosques. In this way, it was thought, people would see that Islam had conquered Christianity. Different countries designed their mosques in different styles, though very many of them included domes and halls and courtyards with pillars. The outsides of mosques were usually plain. But inside there were often superb designs in tiles and mosaics, and fine carpets for the congregation to kneel on as they prayed.

An Arab market spice seller. The trade in spices from the Far East was always important and brought great profits. Some spices were, quite literally, worth their weight in gold. Crusaders fighting in the Holy Land soon got a taste for spices and their use spread through Europe.

Camels are still used to carry goods in Islamic lands, since they can travel great distances across the desert without drinking.

men in different states to exchange goods, or the knowledge of how to produce them.

Before the time of Islam, Syria was part of the Byzantine empire and the rival Sassanid dynasty ruled the lands farther east. The story was told then of a Christian monk who introduced the knowledge of silk-making from Sassanid territory into Syria. He had to smuggle

Trade

Merchants traded freely throughout the Islamic world, using a common currency.

Luxuries and vital goods were spread throughout the Islamic world by trade and by the use of huge quantities of gold. In the centuries before the Islamic conquest, states around the Mediterranean and in the Near East had often been jealous and hostile towards one another. Because of this, it had frequently been difficult or dangerous for

In this picture of the Turkish town of Ankara, painted in the 18th century, the square is lined with the little booths where merchants carried out their business. In the background a caravan of camels sets out on a trading journey. Merchants might be away for many months, and their caravans were often attacked by bandits.

the living silkworms across the frontier, hiding them in a hollow stick. The Sassanid rulers did not want the Byzantines to be able to produce silk. If the monk had been caught he would have been severely punished.

Trading with ease
When the Islamic empire was set up, trading became much easier and less dangerous. Goods could be carried over a vast area, stretching from the Near East to Spain, without passing a single hostile frontier. The spread of the Arabic language meant that buyers and sellers found it possible to understand and to trust one another, even when they came from different countries. A single type of gold coin, the *dinar*, was used throughout Muslim lands. So traders who went to distant Islamic countries did not have to worry about being paid in foreign coins which they could not use at home.

Vast supplies of gold came into Muslim hands. It was not used merely for ornament; much of it was made into coins and put to work. It bought goods from many countries. These goods in turn were often used to help increase the wealth of the country which bought them. Muslim Egypt, for example, was so short of wood that the government tried to keep a record of every tree in the country to prevent timber being wasted.

Below: This Turkish dish has a wave-like design round its border. It is taken from Chinese designs and reminds us how contact through trade helped to spread ideas from one country to another.

31

Egyptian gold was therefore used to buy timber from India, and from the traders of Venice, in north-eastern Italy. Some of the imported timber was then used in Egypt to line the water channels which helped crops to grow. Wood also heated the Egyptian kilns which produced pottery and glass.

Travellers stopped for the night at 'caravanserais', which provided them with lodgings and gave them some protection from raiders. The 19th-century print above shows a caravanserai crowded with all sorts of travellers, from rich nobles to humble traders. Below: Ruins of a caravanserai in Iran.

Still more wood was used in Egypt for ship-building. Merchant ships were needed for more trading; fighting vessels were built to protect the coasts and the merchant ships. The Christian rulers of the Byzantine empire strongly disapproved of Venice selling timber to the Muslims. Some of it would be used to build ships to fight the Byzantines themselves. So when the Byzantines captured a ship-load of timber bound for Egypt or North Africa, they burned it. But still the trade went on. The lure of Muslim gold was hard to resist.

Trading by caravan

Long-distance trading was also carried out over land. Camels, donkeys, horses, or mules were roped together to form a *caravan*, a small procession of animals loaded with goods for sale. These caravans travelled between Islamic towns, and into non-Islamic countries. The animals and the men driving them needed rest and refreshment as they journeyed. So *caravanserais* were built along the main trading routes. These were groups of buildings where travellers could wash, rest, and find some food. Sometimes a caravanserai contained a mosque or even a small hospital. It must have been a happy moment for a trader, tired after crossing miles of desert under

a harsh sun, when a caravanserai came into sight.

Islamic trade brought new and important products from east to west. Silk-making, an art which had once been so dangerous to transport, now spread easily from one Muslim land to another. From Syria it was introduced to Sicily and Spain. Cotton plants were brought westwards, from Mesopotamia to Syria, now that both areas were under the same government. Cloth from Mosul in northern Mesopotamia, and from Damascus, became internationally famous for its high quality. Even in the Christian lands of western Europe they were so familiar that types of cloth are still known there as 'muslin' (from Mosul) and 'damask' (from Damascus).

Syria also became famous for its fine glassware, and for its sugary goods. Fruit grown in the fertile area around Damascus was preserved in Syrian sugar and sold internationally. The habit of eating a sweet course at the end of a meal was introduced into Europe from the Islamic east. Sugar cane was grown especially in Mesopotamia. Transparent brown sugar was first produced in Egypt: it was called *qand* in Arabic from which comes the word 'candy'. The word 'sugar' also comes from an Arabic word, *assokhar*. In Egypt, sugar was so plentiful that during festivals huge numbers of little figures made of sugar were used to decorate the trees.

Adding up on paper

Muslim traders brought two other important skills into the Mediterranean lands. One was the making of paper, and the other the use of Arabic numbers. Paper-making, long known in China, is said to have been learned by eastern Muslims from Chinese prisoners-of-war. By AD 800, officials in Baghdad had begun to use paper for their records. They gave up the earlier writing materials of parchment, which was made from sheepskin, and papyrus, which was made from the pressed fibres of a marsh plant. Records kept on paper were more trustworthy. Dishonest officials could

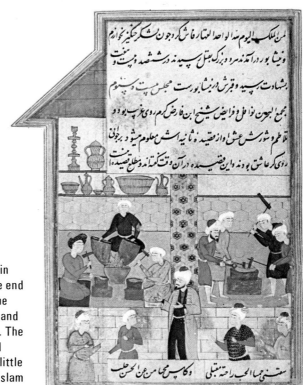

A brass beater's shop in Shiraz, in Persia, at the end of the 16th century. The brass wares are made and sold in the same place. The shapes of the pots and vessels have changed little from the early days of Islam until the present day.

scrape or wash away part of a message or instruction written on parchment or papyrus, and write new words of their own without leaving any revealing traces. But on paper this was impossible. Paper, made from flax or hemp, came to be used throughout the Muslim world in the 9th and 10th centuries.

From India Muslim traders learned a very convenient way of writing numbers. This used nine digits and the nought. It was the same system that we have today. Earlier ways of writing numbers had been very clumsy. For instance the number 'three hundred and eighty eight', which the Muslims now learned to write as 388, had been written in the old Roman numbers as CCCLXXXVIII. The new way of writing numbers also made it easy to add and subtract in columns. From the middle of the 9th century the new system spread through the Islamic world. Later it reached Christian Europe. Although this way of numbering came originally from India, it became known in Christian countries as 'Arabic', because it was brought to Europe by Muslim traders and scholars who wrote in Arabic.

In the windy lands of Afghanistan and eastern Persia much larger towers were built to stand on their own. They trapped the wind in a similar way, and used its force to turn a great screw inside the tower. The screw drove machinery which worked large millstones. When grain was put between the millstones it could be ground into flour by the force of the wind. In Morocco, Egypt, and Spain windmills like this also ground up sugar cane. Muslim countries used windmills long before they were used in Europe.

Water under the desert

The more food that could be grown in an area, the larger the number of people who could be kept alive. Water was even more important than wind for the production of food. In Muslim lands there were vast and successful schemes for watering dry soil so that crops could grow. Channels were built, sometimes 80 kilometres (50 miles) long, to bring water from the hills to the desert plains. Bringing water in this way is known as irrigation. If water in a hot country is brought overground, the heat of the sun turns much of it into vapour, which is then lost in the atmosphere. This is called evaporation. So in Persia, to prevent this from happening, a system of channels was built deep underground. The channels, called *qanats*, were begun before the Muslim conquest, and were developed and extended by the Muslims. The qanats greatly helped the prosperity of Persia because more crops could be grown. When the invader Timur the Lame (also called Tamerlane) destroyed

Wind and Water

Wind towers like these, in south Arabia, were built to bring cooling breezes down into houses.

Both wind and water were widely used to improve living conditions.

In the hot dry lands near the Mediterranean, the power of wind and water can save lives when it is cleverly used. It can also bring comforts and luxury. Muslim builders used the wind to protect themselves from the heat. On top of houses they erected small towers with vents. These towers trapped the cool breezes, which blew in through the vents and were then directed down into the houses. Towers like this can still be seen in Islamic countries.

BLOWING AWAY SAND

The wind often blew sand in from the desert. This piled up on top of fertile earth, and prevented food from being grown. But Muslim farmers had learned to use the wind itself to defeat this process. When sand piled up, a low wall was built behind it. Then in front of the sand, on the side facing the wind, high screens of matting were built, with a gap open at the base. The wind roaring in through the gap was trapped between the matting and the wall, and turned into a little whirlwind. The unwanted sand was caught up in the whirlwind, and blown away.

many of the qanats in AD 1384, the wealth of the country immediately began to decline.

Measuring the flood

In Egypt, since very ancient times, the yearly flooding of the river Nile had fertilized a large area of land. The greater the flood, the larger was the area of land made fertile, and the bigger the crop. Muslim rulers of Egypt were anxious to know just how great the flood was each year. If they knew this, they could also tell how much tax the farmers would be able to pay. So in the 860s they built a tower, called the Nilometer, to measure the Nile flood. A skilled mathematician helped to construct it, and measurements were marked up its side. Water from the Nile entered the tower at three levels. The deeper the Nile flood was, the farther up the tower the water was forced. By seeing how far up the tower the water came, the government of Egypt knew how deep the flood was, how big the crop would be, and how much tax to demand from the farmers.

New crops for Spain

In Spain, perhaps the greatest achievement of the Muslim conquerors was to make large districts fertile. They brought water to dry areas of southern Spain, and so they made it possible for crops from other parts of the world to be produced there for the first time. Bananas, oranges, sugar cane, rice, and cotton were now grown. Sadly, after the Spanish Muslims had been conquered by Christians in the late Middle Ages, Christian rulers chose to wreck the precious Muslim irrigation system, rather than learn how to use it.

In the towns of Islam much money was spent on providing plentiful water. In Samarkand in the Muslim east, and at Fez in North Africa, pipes and channels brought water running through the streets into private houses. This was a luxury unknown in much of the world: most people still had to bring water by hand from a river or a spring. At Fez on summer evenings the running water was diverted to clean the market place.

Cleanliness is believed by Muslims to be an important part of religion. Fountains were provided in mosques, so that worshippers could wash before praying. Fountains were also built in the elegant gardens of the rich. When a person had crossed the scorched deserts which surrounded many Muslim towns, it was a wonderful relief to enter a colourful garden with cool water. Much money was therefore spent in making elaborate and beautiful private gardens. Even in Paradise good Muslims expected to enjoy a fertile garden with fountains playing in the sun.

Great wooden waterwheels on the river Orontes in Syria. The force of the river turned the wheel, which scooped up water on little paddles and carried it to the top, where it was emptied into an aqueduct (left). The water was carried away to irrigate the fields.

Baghdad, capital of the 'Abbasid caliphs, was famous for beauty and luxury. But much of it was destroyed in 1258 by the Mongols. This painting of 1468 shows the river Tigris in flood at Baghdad.

Baghdad

Under its 'Abbasid rulers the city of Baghdad was famous for beauty and luxury.

When they had destroyed the Umayyads of Damascus, the new 'Abbasid rulers of the Islamic empire decided to build a safe and impressive new capital city of their own. Baghdad, in Iraq, was the site they chose. There the great rivers Tigris and Euphrates ran closely together and gave protection against enemies. The site was also convenient for trade. Merchants could sail down the Tigris from Baghdad to the Arabian Gulf, and then across the sea to India and China. Since the Euphrates flows from Syria, other traders could bring goods from there down river to Baghdad. Beginning in 762, the caliph al-Mansur built massive circular walls at Baghdad for its defence. Inside he built his palace. Within a few years the city had spread far beyond the walls. By AD 800 it probably had nearly two million inhabitants. No other city in the world had so many.

We know little about the lives of the poor, who made up most of the population of the city, but the splendour of the 'Abbasid court was famous, and information about it still survives. The caliph Harun ar-Rashid, who ruled from AD 786 to 809, had a yearly income from taxes of about 150 million gold dinars. This was a huge sum, and ten times as much as the caliph was getting a hundred years later. Among the treasures of the court was a large artificial tree, made of silver. In its branches sat mechanical birds, which sang when driven by water or the wind.

Scholars and scientists

Some of the wealth of Baghdad was used to encourage learning. Clever men were paid to come to the city, sometimes even from the Byzantine empire. Although Byzantine Greeks were seen as enemies, many Muslims realized that the Byzantines possessed important information

When the 'Abbasid al-Ma'mun married a lady named Buran at Baghdad, he gave her presents which were famous for centuries afterwards. Buran was given 1000 rubies, and carpets were laid down for her which were decorated with threads of gold, and with rubies and pearls. During the wedding-feast huge amounts of wood were burned in the palace kitchens. It was said that every day for a year hundreds of mules had arrived bringing the wood. Guests were ferried to the feast by thousands of boats which had gathered on the river Tigris.

The Ottoman Sultan Suleiman crosses to Baghdad. He captured the city in 1534.

which clever Ancient Greeks had discovered. This they were eager to learn. A college for translators was set up at Baghdad. Its members were paid to translate into Arabic the writings of Greeks and other foreigners. Many of the caliph's subjects then learnt what Ancient Greeks had known about medicine and mechanics, astronomy and mathematics. By adding ideas of their own, the scientists of Islam became the best in the world – in some ways even better than the Ancient Greeks. Manuscripts written at Baghdad were sometimes illustrated. Paintings produced for this purpose are some of the most attractive works of art surviving from the city.

Enemies

The caliphs had many enemies who wanted to take away their wealth and power. To frighten these enemies, and to get confessions from them, a great torture chamber was built at Baghdad. It was often used. Many spies were employed to watch for enemies. Even high government officials were watched by the caliph's spies. One spy reported that the governor of Baghdad was not working hard enough. Instead, he was spending most of his time with a beautiful slave girl!

A postal service was set up in Iraq, and its main job was to carry the reports of spies. From the early 9th century pigeons were used to bring the post. The main post office in Baghdad contained much information about travelling in the caliph's lands. Traders and pilgrims were allowed to use it to plan their journeys.

In spite of their efforts, the caliphs gradually lost power, even in Baghdad itself. In 1258 invading Mongols killed the last 'Abbasid caliph, and wrecked much of his city. No one else was appointed caliph of Baghdad, although it remained a trade centre. It was overrun by the Mongols in 1258 and again in 1401. Lying between the Persian and Turkish empires, it changed hands a number of times between them. In the 18th century it at last became great and powerful again, and in 1921 Baghdad became a capital once more – this time of the new country of Iraq.

The madrasa Mulaniyah at Baghdad. Madrasas were teaching colleges; Baghdad was famous as a centre of learning.

Spain

For some 800 years much of Spain was ruled by Muslims. They brought prosperity and learning.

Among the few gardens that have survived from early times is this beautiful court in the Alhambra, the great Muslim palace at Granada in Spain. Water arches across the long pool from rows of fountains, behind which are beds of bushes. It was built in the 14th century AD. The Alhambra was a fortress as well as the home of the ruler. It was the last Muslim stronghold in Spain to surrender to the Christians.

In the early 700s southern Spain was conquered by Muslim troops, coming from North Africa. At first the conquered territory was ruled by Umayyad caliphs in distant Damascus. In 750 most of the Umayyads in Syria were slaughtered (see page 13). In the east, the power of their clan was finished. But one Umayyad prince, ʿAbd ar-Rahman, managed to escape. He fled far to the west to Spain. There he became ruler, and Umayyad relatives of his ruled after him. Their capital was the city of Cordoba.

Spain prospers

Gold from West Africa helped Muslim Spain to become wealthy. The rulers of Cordoba controlled much of the African gold trade. Some of the gold was used by Spanish Muslims to buy slaves from eastern Europe. These slaves were resold to Muslims in other countries at a large profit. Fine cloth and leather goods were produced in Spanish towns: Cordoba alone is said to have had about 13,000 weavers. Muslim farmers, with their skilful methods of irrigation, cultivated huge new areas of Spain. Enough food was produced to support a large and often prosperous population.

In the 900s Cordoba and its suburbs had about half a million inhabitants, far more than any other city of western Europe at that time. In other European cities the streets were made of earth, and were often muddy and very dark at night. But at Cordoba streets were paved and had lighting. Beautifully coloured tiles were used to decorate the walls of rooms in important buildings. Many schools and a university were set up. High wages were offered to attract good teachers and writers from other Muslim lands.

Muslim Spain led Europe in many ways. It was the first European territory to use paper. The knowledge of how to make paper had been brought to Spain from the Muslim east. From Spain it was passed to Christian Europe. The making of sugary delicacies such as marzipan and nougat were introduced to Europe through Muslim Spain. Sherry, one of the finest wines in the world, was made from a type of grape from Persia and grown at Jerez de la Frontera in Muslim Spain. The musicians of Spain were famous internationally. The guitar was first brought to Spain by Muslim musicians. Spanish guitarists were eventually to become the best in the world.

Fighting for Spain

Part of northern Spain was never conquered by the Muslims and remained under Christian rule. Where the Christian and Muslim areas met, fighting was common. One Muslim ruler of Cordoba, al-

Nearly all the mosques of Islamic Spain were destroyed by Christians. But the Great Mosque at Cordoba escaped, though it was turned into a Christian church. This is the 'mihrab', a recess in the wall facing the direction of Mecca. The round horseshoe arch is often found in Muslim architecture.

A carved box from 10th-century Islamic Spain. It is made from ivory. The Arabic lettering around the lid spells out the name of the son of a ruler of Cordoba.

Mansur, invaded northern Spain, and demolished the famous Christian shrine of Santiago de Compostela. He returned to Cordoba in triumph, bringing the doors and bells of the destroyed building. Christians were furious. After al-Mansur died, in 1002, one Christian monk wrote angrily in his chronicle, 'In this year died al-Mansur, and was buried in Hell'. But al-Mansur himself had been very proud of fighting for Islam. He collected the dust which had gathered on his coat-of-mail during years of fighting against Christians and arranged for it to be buried close to him when he died.

After al-Mansur's death Cordoba was less important. Before AD 1100 Spanish Islam was divided into several kingdoms. One by one they were conquered by Christians from the north. The last to be captured was Granada, where one of the most beautiful palaces in the world had been built. It was known as the Alhambra.

After the Christian conquest important books from the Islamic world were translated in Spain, by Muslims and especially by Jews. The writings of excellent Muslim scientists, and of the Ancient Greek thinker Aristotle, were translated into Latin, the language of the Roman Catholic Church in Christian Europe. So thanks to the Jewish and Muslim translators, educated Christians in Europe were at last able to learn about these authors.

Medicine and Science

Islamic scholars and scientists learned from the civilizations they conquered, and added to this knowledge by their own work.

The Muslims did not look down on the knowledge of other peoples. Instead, they were eager to learn from them. In the 8th and 9th centuries scientific books by Ancient Greeks were collected and translated into Arabic. Many of the books were unknown in Europe after the fall of the Roman empire, and much later on had to be translated again, this time from Arabic into Latin, so that European scholars could learn from them.

The scientists of Islam did not only learn from books. In the 12th century a famous doctor, 'Abd al-Latif, made important discoveries about the shape of human bones by digging up skeletons from an Ancient Egyptian graveyard.

Some Muslims believed that diseases were sent by Allah, to punish sins. But the 14th-century doctor Ibn al-Khatib disagreed. He noticed how diseases spread when sick people came close to

Astronomers in an observatory at Istanbul (Constantinople) in the 16th century. Among the instruments they hold is a circular astrolabe. This was used for measuring the position of planets and stars. Islamic astronomers learned from Persians, Syrians, and Greeks. They added to this store of knowledge by their own observations.

others. People in a sea-port fell ill after sick men from a ship had landed there. It seemed to Ibn al-Khatib that disease came from infection, and not from Allah.

Mathematics and chemistry

The mathematicians of Islam were also famous. They invented the science of algebra: the word 'algebra' itself comes from the Arab word *al-jabr*. The knowledge of chemistry was greatly advanced by scientists in the Islamic world. In earlier times scientists had usually not understood how important experiments were for discovering information, but now many useful experiments were carried out. Often scientists were hoping to make gold. These alchemists, as they were called, never succeeded, but through their experiments they did find much important information about chemistry, even though they could not make gold.

After AD 1100 the Islamic world produced fewer new ideas than before. Strict Muslims came to believe that adventurous thinking was making people disbelieve the Koran. So scientific investigation and other study were discouraged.

A page from a 13th-century astronomical book showing the constellations Hercules and Lyra.

DOCTORS IN ISLAM
The Muslims had skilled doctors. Some of them trained at special centres such as the House of Wisdom in Baghdad which was set up in the 9th century by the Caliph al-Ma'mun. Many learned books were written about diseases. The *Canon of Medicine* by the Persian doctor Ibn Sina (often called by his Latin name Avicenna) became the chief guide for medical students in Europe from the 12th to the 17th centuries.

Many doctors had to pass exams before they could practice, and had to be skilled in the use of medicines. In remote areas doctors travelled by camel to reach sick people.

The Legacy

In Africa and Asia, Islamic power grew. But the Muslims were driven out of Spain and the Turkish invasion of central Europe failed.

In the centuries after the fall of the 'Abbasid caliphate (see page 13), the power of Islam grew. Turkish Muslims captured Asia Minor from the Byzantines, and eventually conquered Constantinople itself in AD 1453. The great city became the capital of the Ottoman Turks. Their empire spread far into south-eastern Europe. In 1529, and again in 1683, Turkish troops reached as far west as Vienna in Austria. The great Turkish empire in Europe and the Near East lasted until the 19th and early 20th centuries. In India, too, Islamic rulers called 'Mughals' controlled a vast area from the 16th to the 19th century.

Nowadays Islam stretches from northern Africa and the Near East to Pakistan and Bangladesh in the Indian sub-continent. There are other Muslim communities in Indonesia and Malaya, and in parts of China and the USSR. Many Muslims today keep closely to their traditional way of life.

Muslims in Europe

In Spain, Islam was less fortunate. When Granada surrendered in 1492, the Christian conquerors promised to allow the Muslims to go on practising their religion. This promise was broken. Mosques were destroyed, and Arabic books were burnt. Many Muslims were murdered, and almost all the survivors were forced to leave Spain in 1609. The number of Muslims killed or driven out may have been about 3 million.

However, the effects of Islam on Europe have been long-lasting. European schools and universities in the Middle Ages were greatly improved by the learning brought from Islamic lands.

The use of paper and of Arabic numbers came to Europe from Islam, as we have seen. The stained-glass windows of medieval churches, and the cool many-coloured tiles still used in Spain resulted from copying Islamic art.

When new products and ideas reached Europe from Islam, they often went on being called by an Arabic name. Sugar, syrup, and coffee came to Europe in this way, and their names all come from Arabic. Some Arabic words were brought to Europe by traders in strange and interesting ways – like the word 'tabby', which is now used for cats. A prince of Baghdad was called 'Attab, and the district where he lived was named after him. Striped cloth was made in this district, and so was called ''Attabi'. Muslim traders sold cloth like this in Europe. Its name changed slightly to 'tabi' or 'tabby', and was used for anything with stripes. So nowadays, when we call a striped cat a 'tabby', when we use Arabic numbers and write on paper, drink coffee and use sugar, we are doing things which our ancestors learned many centuries ago from the great civilization of Islam.

The painted pottery from Iznik in Asia Minor made Ottoman art valued all over the world. This Iznik plate dates from the 16th century.

The Ottoman Sultan Suleiman expanded his empire far into eastern Europe. Here he besieges Bucharest, in modern Romania.

Glossary

'Abbasids Caliphs who ruled at Baghdad from 750 to 1258. They were descended from an uncle of Muhammad.

Al-, ar-, as- The Arabic for 'the'.

Allah The name given by the Muslims to God alone, who revealed his message, the Koran, to Muhammad.

Astrolabe An instrument used by the Muslims to measure the position of stars and planets, to cast horoscopes, and to tell the time.

Bazaar A large market area, often roofed over, in which traders sell their wares from booths.

Bedouin Tribal nomads of Arabian origin, who since before the time of Muhammad have moved around in search of grazing for their flocks and herds.

Caliph The head of the Muslim community. The Ummayad and 'Abbasid caliphs were powerful rulers. In later times power passed to viziers, but the caliph remained the religious head of the community.

Caravanserai A lodging place for travellers, particularly merchants, also known as a khan or rubat. Some caravanserais had special quarters for government officials and provisions for trading.

Byzantine The name used for the Eastern Roman Empire, with its capital at Constantinople (Byzantium). When Islam arose, the Byzantine empire controlled Asia Minor, much of North Africa, and the Near East. The Muslims soon gained control of Syria, Palestine, Egypt, and North Africa, leaving the Byzantines only Asia Minor, and eventually only Constantinople itself. Even this was finally conquered by the Muslims in 1453.

Gabriel Muslims believe that the angel Gabriel was Allah's messenger to Muhammad.

Hadith or Tradition The sayings and deeds of Muhammad, collected after his death. The Hadith is second in importance and authority only to the Koran.

Hajj The pilgrimage to Mecca which every Muslim who can afford to should make at least once in his or her lifetime.

Harem The private quarters of a house, in which the women live.

Hijra Muhammad's journey from Mecca to Medina in AD 622. This year is taken as Year One of the Muslim calendar.

Imam The spiritual leader of the Islamic community. The term can be used either for the caliph, or head of the whole Islamic community, or for the leader of the prayers in a mosque.

Janissaries Slaves who were converted to Islam as boys and formed into the Turkish sultan's main bodyguard. They became immensely powerful until they were finally overthrown in the mid-19th century.

Ka'ba The most sacred place of worship of the Muslims at Mecca. It is a cube-shaped building covered with a black veil. Inside is the Black Stone (possibly a meteorite) closely associated with Abraham. It is also called Baituldah (the House of God). Every Muslim faces the direction of the Ka'ba when he prays.

Koran The holy book of the Muslims, containing the message of Allah as it was revealed to Muhammad.

Mamluks A dynasty of freed slaves who ruled in Egypt and Syria from 1250 to 1517. They were mainly Turkish in origin.

Mihrab A recess or slab in a place of prayer which indicates the direction of Mecca, which people praying should face.

Minaret The tower from which Muslims are called to prayer five times each day.

Minbar A platform in a mosque, placed to the right of the mihrab, used by the preacher.

Mongols People from the steppes of Central Asia who led a nomadic life and at times ruled over large

Left: A Bedouin and his camel. In the background is the tent in which he lives.

The mihrab of the mosque of Sultan Muaiyad, built in Cairo in the early 15th century. The mihrab was a recess in a wall facing in the direction of Mecca, and was especially beautifully decorated. This one is made of marble.

such as marriages are seldom held there, no statues or pictures decorate it, and there is no music or singing. A mosque also serves as a school and court.

Muezzin A man whose duty it is to give the call to prayer five times each day.

Mughals (Moguls) Muslim rulers of India, descended from the Mongol Timur the Lame (Tamerlane). They ruled over northern India from the 16th to the late 18th century. They are particularly remembered for the beautiful painting and buildings produced under their rule.

Muhtasib An inspector of market weights and measures and cleanliness. He was also a powerful critic of public behaviour – a sort of moral policeman. He often had the powers of a magistrate.

Ottomans Turkish rulers who became increasingly powerful from the 14th century on. In 1453 they captured Constantinople (Byzantium) which was renamed Istanbul and which became the capital of a vast empire. The Ottoman empire finally collapsed only in the 20th century.

Ramadan The ninth month of the Muslim lunar year. During Ramadan Muslims must not eat, drink, or smoke from dawn until nightfall.

Seljuks Turkish rulers powerful in the 11th to 13th centuries, when they controlled Central Asia and Iraq.

This mosaic decorates the Great Mosque at Damascus. It was made in the early 8th century. At this time Muslim art still looked much like that of the eastern Roman or Byzantine empire.

The Ottoman Sultan Mehemmed II under whom Constantinople was captured in 1453.

Sultan The independent ruler of a territory. The early Ottoman rulers also called themselves sultans.

Umayyads Caliphs who reigned from 661 to 750, when they were overthrown by the 'Abbasids. They then set up a caliphate in Spain, where they ruled until 1031.

Vizier An important court official who, under the Seljuks, Mongols and Ottomans was often the ruler's deputy.

areas. They were often in conflict with the Muslims, particularly in the 13th century under Genghis Khan. Baghdad fell to the Mongols in 1258. Many of the Mongols were converted to Islam.

Mosque A formal place of prayer and worship for Muslims. It contains a mihrab and minbar, and a minaret is often attached to it. It is very different from a Christian church; ceremonies

The dome of a mosque at Mashad, in Iran. On either side are two slender minarets from which Muslims are called to prayer each day by the muezzin.

Index

Bold entries indicate a major mention.
Italic numerals indicate an illustration.

*paintings are reproduced throughout the book and text entries only are indexed

ACKNOWLEDGEMENTS

Photographs: Half title Victoria & Albert Museum, London; contents page Victoria & Albert Museum, London (top and centre), ZEFA (bottom); page 7 Victoria & Albert Museum, London (top), ZEFA (bottom); 8 British Museum; 9 Victoria & Albert Museum, London; 10 Sonia Halliday; 11 Sonia Halliday (top), Bibliothèque Nationale, Paris (bottom); 12 British Museum; 13 A. Hornak; 16 Victoria & Albert Museum, London (top), British Museum (bottom); 17 Victoria & Albert Museum, London (top), A. Hutchinson (bottom); 18, 19 British Museum; 20 Sonia Halliday (top), A. Hutchinson/Clark (bottom); 22 Bibliothèque Nationale, Paris (top), Sonia Halliday (bottom); Bibliothèque Nationale, Paris (top), British Library (bottom); 24 British Library (top and centre), British Museum (bottom); 25 Bibliothèque Nationale, Paris (top), Sonia Halliday (bottom); 26 Bibliothèque Nationale, Paris; 27 Sonia Halliday; 28 Michael Holford (top), Victoria & Albert Museum, London (bottom); 29 British Museum (top), ZEFA (bottom); 30 Sonia Halliday; 31 Rijksmuseum, Amsterdam (top), Victoria & Albert Museum, London (bottom); 32 Sonia Halliday (top), ZEFA (bottom); 33 British Museum; 34 ZEFA; 35 Sonia Halliday; 36 British Museum; 37 Sonia Halliday (top), Robert Harding Associates (bottom); 38 ZEFA; 39 Sonia Halliday (top), Louvre, Paris (bottom); 40 British Museum; 41 British Museum (top), Sonia Halliday (bottom); 42 Sonia Halliday; 43 A. Hornak (top left), Sonia Halliday (top right), Robert Harding Associates (bottom left), A Hornak (bottom right).

Picture research : Jackie Cookson

AD 550	**ISLAM**	**EUROPE**

AD 550

ISLAM

571 Muhammad is born in Mecca

622 Muhammad and his followers move
to Medina (the *Hijra*)

630 The Muslims return to Mecca
which becomes the centre of Islam
632 Death of Muhammad
633 Muslims conquer Syria and Iraq
639 Muslims begin the conquest of
Egypt

640 Persia (Iran) comes under Muslim
rule

700

711 Spain and the Indus Valley are
invaded by the Muslims

762 Baghdad becomes the 'Abbasid'
capital

970 The Seljuk Turks become Muslims
and occupy most of Persia

1000

1055 The Seljuks seize Baghdad

1379 Timur the Lame (Tamerlane)
invades Persia

1453 Ottoman Turks capture
Constantinople (Byzantium) which
becomes their capital
1492 Granada falls to Christians

1490

EUROPE

590–604 Gregory I, the Great, Pope
597 St Augustine lands in England
620 Vikings begin invading Ireland

732 Muslims defeated at the battle of
Poitiers by the Franks

771–814 Charlemagne, King of the
Franks
861 Vikings discover Iceland
871–899 Alfred the Great, King of
Wessex

1066 Battle of Hastings

1152–1190 Frederick I, Holy Roman
Emperor

1241 Mongols withdraw from Europe

1348–1351 Black Death ravages Europe

1431 Jeanne d'Arc
burned as a witch
1453 End of Hundred
Years' War